SURE & STEADY

LEARNING AND GROWING
IN PASTORAL MINISTRY

ED TAYLOR

SURE & STEADY:
LEARNING AND GROWING IN PASTORAL MINISTRY

By Ed Taylor
Copyright ©2021 by Ed Taylor
Published by ABOUNDING GRACE MEDIA
ISBN: 978-0-9965723-4-7

ABOUNDING GRACE MEDIA
18900 E. Hampden Ave., Aurora, CO 80013
(303) 628-7200

A B O U N D I N G   G R A C E
MEDIA GROUP™

LEARNING AND GROWING IN PASTORAL MINISTRY

TABLE OF CONTENTS:

4

LEARNING AND GROWING IN PASTORAL MINISTRY

Over the past 25 years of pastoral ministry, I've had the privilege of failing, stumbling, and learning along the way. Looking back, I wish someone would have handed me a book or pamphlet to help me prepare for the many things I would face. But along the way, I learned as many people do, "the hard way". I want to help you learn a little differently.

The work of the pastor is often varied and unpredictable. It can be very repetitive and mundane, or it can be very dynamic and wild! Learning to apply yourself will bless you, bless your church, bless your community, and ultimately bless the Lord! As you choose to abide in Jesus, He supplies everything you need to fulfill God's high call upon your life.

The book in your hand is an ongoing project. It's impossible to capture the true essence of ministry as every person and situation is different but we've tried to capture a few of the key ingredients that make for a strong and growing leader in God's Church. The project started with me writing down some initial thoughts. Then, on a Wednesday morning in 2021, our pastoral team here at Calvary spent hours together collaborating and editing these entries with the hope of encouraging you on the path of your spiritual leadership, no matter what the role may be. The focus is on the work of an assistant pastor. However, the applications are deep and wide, applicable to any leadership role in the Church. I hope to encourage, instruct, and exhort you to yield yourself fully to the Lord in your pastoral and leadership calling. I am asking you to take it seriously and desire to grow in your under- standing of how God wants to use you.

May the Lord bless you in His work!

My personal email is ed@edtaylor.org and my cell is 720-608-0012. If I can help serve you, reach out to me any time.

1 Timothy 3:1 (NKJV) "This is a faithful saying: If a man desires the position of a bishop (episkopes), he desires a good work."

HOW TO USE THIS BOOK:

There are several ways this book can be an effective discipleship tool for you and others. As you read through the series of topics, know that God will use them to stimulate your prayer life and stir up a desire to grow in His grace. In order to maximize your time, you can use this book in at least three different ways.

1. **PERSONAL DEVOS:** Use it as a daily devotional, taking notes along the way as the Lord encourages you.

2. **GROUP DISCUSSION:** Use it as a discipleship tool through group discussion. Read the topic and discuss within your leadership team, clarifying along the way how the particular topic applies in the local context of your ministry.

3. **SMALL GROUP STUDY:** Use it as a small group study covering many topics a night. Discussions and note taking will help solidify the lessons learned.

However you choose to use it, may the Lord help you grow in becoming the servant/leader He desires.

1. PERSONAL RELATIONSHIP W/ JESUS:
A pastor has a strong relationship with Jesus.

A pastor must have an internal, growing relationship with Jesus Christ. The beginning of any ministry venture is the love of God. Without a love relationship with Jesus, the ministry is simply a job, something to do, something to get done. Without first having that abiding presence of a true love toward God upwardly, it's impossible to be a vessel of love toward others outwardly.The vertical love for God occurs first, then our horizontal love for each other follows.

Our essence of existing is the love of God poured out upon us, not when we were at our best, but when we were at our worst. The love of God is the very glue that holds our relationship together, growing us in grace, extending our hearts toward Him and others.

God has created a pastor's position out of His love for you and His love for the flock. When times get tough, we have the love of God steadily stabilizing us. When all looks bleak, we have the love of God sustaining us. God loves us through our doubts. The love of God keeps us strong even when we waver. When we don't know what to do, the love of God is the anchor that brings us back to wisdom.

Before you step out in answering the call of ministry, reassess your love relationship with God through Jesus Christ. This regular reassessment occurs over and over again throughout our life of ministry and service.

Scriptures to consider:

John 3:3 (NKJV) *"Jesus answered and said to him, "Most assuredly, I say to you, unless one is born again, he cannot see the kingdom of God.""*

John 15:4 (NKJV) *"Abide in Me, and I in you. As the branch cannot bear fruit of itself, unless it abides in the vine, neither can you, unless you abide in Me."*

2 Peter 1:10 (NKJV) *"Therefore, brethren, be even more diligent to make your call and election sure, for if you do these things you will never stumble;"*

1 John 1:3 (NKJV) *"that which we have seen and heard we declare to you, that you also may have fellowship with us; and truly our fellowship is with the Father and with His Son Jesus Christ."*

LEARNING AND GROWING IN PASTORAL MINISTRY

PERSONALLY FILLED WITH THE HOLY SPIRIT: A pastor has been baptized with the Holy Spirit for fruitful service.

A pastor's relationship with the Holy Spirit is fundamental for ministry. Not only is he in-dwelt by the Spirit, but he must be baptized by the Holy Spirit as well. Jesus promised the baptism of the Holy Spirit to those who asked for it. With the baptism of the Holy Spirit in a pastor's life, supernatural power is given to him to be a witness. It is impossible to serve God in the strength of human wisdom, man-centered programs, or from a position of the flesh. While you may be able to get things done, they won't be done in, from, and through His Spirit. A pastor cannot give out what he himself does not posess. A daily, regular filling of His Spirit will enable the pastor to cooperate with all that God desires to accomplish through him. Serving God in your own strength will lead to burnout, weariness, and feelings of being overwhelmed. Serving God in the Spirit is the antidote for these difficult seasons in a pastor's life.

Scriptures to consider:

Acts 1:8 (NKJV) "But you shall receive power when the Holy Spirit has come upon you; and you shall be witnesses to Me in Jerusalem, and in all Judea and Samaria, and to the end of the earth."

Acts 4:31 (NKJV) And when they had prayed, the place where they were assembled together was shaken; and they were all filled with the Holy Spirit, and they spoke the word of God with boldness.

Ephesians 5:18-21 (NKJV) And do not be drunk with wine, in which is dissipation; but be filled with the Spirit, speaking to one another in psalms and hymns and spiritual songs, singing and making melody in your heart to the Lord, giving thanks always for all things to God the Father in the name of our Lord Jesus Christ, submitting to one another in the fear of God.

_____

_____

_____

_____

PERSONAL INTEGRITY:
A pastor has a sterling character and unquestionable integrity.

Fidelity, honesty, and internal character are non-negotiables when stepping into the position of pastor. There should be nothing hidden and no known disqualifying behavior in the man's life. A pastor is known as a man of his word. Following the example of Jesus, his "Yes" is a "Yes," and his "No" is a "No." He tells the truth and doesn't lie. He encourages others to live in the truth. When his name is mentioned, there is no hesitation as to whether one can trust him or not. His reputation is that of a man, even though weak and imperfect, is nonetheless dependent upon the Lord. The pattern of his life is one of humility, repentance, and obedience.

When something is delegated or given to a pastor, he follows through promptly and doesn't need constant reminders to take care of things that need to be taken care of.

Scriptures to consider:

Daniel 6:3–5 (NKJV) *"Then this Daniel distinguished himself above the governors and satraps, because an excellent spirit was in him; and the king gave thought to setting him over the whole realm. So the governors and satraps sought to find some charge against Daniel concerning the kingdom; but they could find no charge or fault, because he was faithful; nor was there any error or fault found in him. Then these men said, "We shall not find any charge against this Daniel unless we find it against him concerning the law of his God."*

1 Timothy 3:1–7 (NKJV) *"This is a faithful saying: If a man desires the position of a bishop, he desires a good work. A bishop then must be blameless, the husband of one wife, temperate, sober-minded, of good behavior, hospitable, able to teach; not given to wine, not violent, not greedy for money, but gentle, not quarrelsome, not covetous; one who rules his own house well, having his children in submission with all reverence (for if a man does not know how to rule his own house, how will he take care of the church of God?); not a novice, lest being puffed up with pride he fall into the same condemnation as the devil. Moreover he must have a good testimony among those who are outside, lest he fall into reproach and the snare of the devil."*

_____

_____

_____

_____

_____

_____

_____

_____

_____

_____

_____

_____

_____

_____

_____

4. **PERSONAL LIFE OF DEVOTION WITH THE LORD:**
A pastor has a genuine personal devotional life.

Serving Jesus can be very difficult at times. Ministry flows from our personal, abiding relationship with Jesus. A pastor must have and maintain a full, vibrant, and increasing devotional life. Your life of devotion fastens you to Him and His calling upon your life. Your energy, strength, and spiritual vitality comes from your fellowship with the Lord, not through relationships with others. There is no substitute for your continual abiding. He is our strength.

Scriptures to consider:

Joshua 1:8 (NKJV) *"This Book of the Law shall not depart from your mouth, but you shall meditate in it day and night, that you may observe to do according to all that is written in it. For then you will make your way prosperous, and then you will have good success."*

Psalm 1:2–3 (NKJV) *"But his delight is in the law of the Lord, And in His law he meditates day and night. He shall be like a tree planted by the rivers of water, that brings forth its fruit in its season, Whose leaf also shall not wither; And whatever he does shall prosper."*

_____

_____

_____

_____

_____

_____

_____

LEARNING AND GROWING IN PASTORAL MINISTRY

_____

_____

_____

_____

_____

_____

_____

_____

_____

_____

_____

_____

_____

_____

_____

_____

5. **PERSONALLY TEACHABLE:**
A pastor is always in every way teachable and moldable in the Master's hands.

A pastor never stops learning. He regularly receives the Word from his pastor in the sanctuary with his Bible open and notepad ready. This desire to receive the Word is not only a great example to the congregation, but it's also essential for your personal spiritual growth. If you no longer hear from Jesus through the pastor that He's placed in your life, you will begin to shrivel up spiritually find yourself spiritually dry and distanced. It's a terribly dangerous place to be.

Be careful not to think too highly of yourself. In the Kingdom of God, we are all replaceable. Watch out that you don't become impressed with yourself. When someone praises you, take it and them to Jesus. When someone complains or criticizes, take it and them to Jesus. Thank God daily and serve your heart out. It's important to die to yourself daily. Be alert to those times when you are defensive and resistant to feedback. Crucify your ego and ambition, allowing God to replace them with His humility and spiritual passion. God has called you into the ministry to serve, love, and help others, NOT for them to serve, love, and help you. Deny yourself and take up your cross and follow Jesus. Trust God. He'll supply all of your needs and give you the love and acceptance you need. Humility takes effort. Many pastors begin serving with a heart that is humble but often becomes prideful. Be careful and stay teachable.

Scriptures to consider:

Proverbs 12:1 (NKJV) "Whoever loves instruction loves knowledge, But he who hates correction is stupid."

2 Timothy 3:16 (NKJV) "All Scripture is given by inspiration of God, and is profitable for doctrine, for reproof, for correction, for instruction in righteousness,"

1 Peter 5:5 (NKJV) "Likewise you younger people, submit yourselves to your elders. Yes, all of you be submissive to one another, and be clothed with humility, for "God resists the proud, But gives grace to the humble.""

LEARNING AND GROWING IN PASTORAL MINISTRY

_____

_____

_____

_____

_____

_____

_____

_____

_____

_____

_____

_____

_____

_____

_____

6. PERSONAL PRAYER LIFE:
A pastor has a very vibrant prayer life.

Your prayer life directly affects your behavior. Without the spiritual weapon of prayer, a pastor will simply not make it. Prayer is one of the most vital yet neglected disciplines in a pastor's life. If you don't have a prayer life, repent, and start afresh and anew. Pray for yourself, your family, your church, your pastor, and literally everything! A pastor's ever-growing personal prayer life with Jesus is essential and non-negotiable. Without a growing spiritual abiding prayer life, it's only a matter of time before you're found out or before many are hurt, and you have a sinful blowout that causes great harm to the name of Jesus. A pastor is in the Word and prayer daily, seeking Jesus for his life and his family. He's basking in the grace, love, and mercy of Jesus, enjoying the love that is so readily his. That love is a great motivator in serving Jesus.

You can never do anything to convince God to stop loving you. He will never stop loving you. But you can, through disobedience and sin, put yourself in a place **where you're not enjoying His love.** Beware of sin and compromise. Beware of spiritual game playing. It will ruin you and do significant damage to the name of Jesus through the ministry under your care. Put a guard over your heart and mind. Stay in the Word and in prayer. Remain close to Jesus.

God desires to bless you abundantly and cause your ministry to bear an abundance of fruit. **Let Him bless you by living a pure and godly life so that He can entrust you with more.** Stay broken, humble, and obedient to the Lord. Be willing to do whatever it takes to get back to that place of abiding love in Him, even if it means giving up your 'ministry' to get back to Him!

Scriptures to consider:

1 Thessalonians 5:16–22 (NKJV) "Rejoice always, pray without ceasing, in everything give thanks; for this is the will of God in Christ Jesus for you. Do not quench the Spirit. Do not despise prophecies. Test all things; hold fast what is good. Abstain from every form of evil."

James 5:16 (NKJV) "Confess your trespasses to one another, and pray for one another, that you may be healed. The effective, fervent prayer of a righteous man avails much."

2 Timothy 2:1 (NKJV) "You therefore, my son, be strong in the grace that is in Christ Jesus."

7. PERSONAL SACRIFICE:

A pastor lives a life of personal sacrifice, regularly dying to himself for the sake of others.

A pastor recognizes that there is a cost to serving in ministry. It's important to understand that God does not call you to personal harm or to sacrifice your family on the altar of ministry. But the ministry will cost you. Jesus taught us that in order to follow Him, we must choose, regularly, to deny ourselves. While this is important for a follower of Christ, it's absolutely a requirement for the pastor. Ministry is full of personal sacrifice, the willing surrender of my rights and privileges to Jesus Christ. It's a choice to die to yourself daily. You are in ministry to serve, love, and help others, not for them to serve you. You are in ministry to give, not to get. Be careful with talking about what you deserve. God has given us much grace and not what we deserve!

A big part of serving Jesus is making yourself available. It begins by being available to Jesus, next, your family, then to the congregation, then to your pastor. You can't excel in helping unless you're there, physically, emotionally, and spiritually. As an assistant pastor, your role is to serve and help at a particular congregation. Keep in mind the ministry needs above your own desires. If and when you're not there, whether on vacation, running a ministry errand, on a mission trip, or just at lunch, someone else will need to help pick up the slack in your absence. When it comes to time off and time away, we can become so self-absorbed that we forget the ministry. Ministry doesn't stop while we are away. Be considerate of the needs of those that serve alongside you and those whom you serve alongside. As you plan, don't forget to have someone available to serve in your absence.

Scriptures to consider:

Philippians 2:2–4 (NKJV) *"Fulfill my joy by being like-minded, having the same love, being of one accord, of one mind. Let nothing be done through selfish ambition or conceit, but in lowliness of mind let each esteem others better than himself. Let each of you look out not only for his own interests, but also for the interests of others."*

Ephesians 5:1–2 (NKJV) *"Therefore be imitators of God as dear children. And walk in love, as Christ also has loved us and given Himself for us, an offering and a sacrifice to God for a sweet-smelling aroma."*

2 Timothy 2:3–4 (NKJV) *"You therefore must endure hardship as a good soldier of Jesus Christ. No one engaged in warfare entangles himself with the affairs of this life, that he may please him who enlisted him as a soldier."*

8. PERSONAL FAMILY LIFE:
A pastor serves and loves his family well.

The pastor's family life is vital and important. Your first ministry is to your family. Ministry comes out of the home first, then back into the home. The pastor will lead his family as a model of leading others in the Church family. He will pray with his wife and kids, protect them from evil, and grow his family in loving submission to Jesus. The single man will oversee his home as unto the Lord, wholly devoted to God.

Scripture to consider:

1 Timothy 3:4–5 (NKJV) *"one who rules his own house well, having his children in submission with all reverence (for if a man does not know how to rule his own house, how will he take care of the church of God?);"*

_____

_____

_____

_____

_____

_____

_____

_____

_____

_____

LEARNING AND GROWING IN PASTORAL MINISTRY

_____

_____

_____

_____

_____

_____

_____

_____

_____

_____

_____

_____

_____

_____

PERSONAL CALLING:
A pastor possesses a strong calling from God.

The call of God upon a man is essential in accepting the role of shepherding others. God calls a man to feed, tend, and care for His flock. When asked by others why you are in the ministry, you need to be able to say, "because God told me to"! The call must be accompanied by validation and agreement by the elders of the church and others. This validation means that no man takes this call to ministry upon Himself. It's not done in isolation but within community. It's not enough to say, "God told me to." A pastor must also receive the validation of your church's elders, pastors, and general congregation.

Scriptures to consider:

2 Peter 1:10 (NKJV) *"Therefore, brethren, be even more diligent to make your call and election sure, for if you do these things you will never stumble;"*

2 Timothy 1:5–7 (NKJV) *"When I call to remembrance the genuine faith that is in you, which dwelt first in your grandmother Lois and your mother Eunice, and I am persuaded is in you also. Therefore I remind you to stir up the gift of God which is in you through the laying on of my hands. For God has not given us a spirit of fear, but of power and of love and of a sound mind."*

_____

_____

_____

_____

_____

_____

_____

10. ## CHURCH LIFE INVOLVEMENT:
A pastor is fully a part of the life of the church community he serves.

The pastor is not merely an employee of the church. Sometimes He's working a full-time job outside of the Church that enables him to serve. The pastor is a part of the community of believers in which he serves. He attends church with his family, receives the Word from his pastor, faithfully gives his tithes and offerings, and enjoys the benefits of his heritage as a son of God! A pastor is a part of a local church and an example within that church family.

Scripture to consider:

Acts 2:41–42 (NKJV) *"Then those who gladly received his word were baptized; and that day about three thousand souls were added to them. And they continued steadfastly in the apostles' doctrine and fellowship, in the breaking of bread, and in prayers."*

_____

_____

_____

_____

_____

_____

_____

_____

_____

_____

11. A PASTOR'S HEART:
A pastor cares for what Jesus cares for.

Having the heart of a shepherd (the heart of the Good Shepherd) is needed to care for, love, and tend the flock of God. The key to this is caring. A pastor cares about God, cares for others, and cares for the glory of God! Because of the great love and grace that he has received, a pastor is a vessel of the agape love to others. He is an open channel for God to demonstrate His love and grace over and over again.

Because of his closeness to Jesus, a pastor is not mean-spirited, hateful, selfish, mean, spiteful, or any of those other fleshly characteristics that aren't reflective of God's unending love and grace. A pastor is a constant source of encouragement, love, and joy to those in the congregation. Be careful not to forget about those that are serving: answering the phones, sweeping, cleaning, preparing food, and tending to their crying kids. As a pastor, you can create a loving environment in the ministry by encouraging folks throughout the day, praying with them, checking in on them, and pastoring all whom you come in contact with.

Make the ministry a happy, joy-filled place where people come to find refuge from their crazy pressure-packed lives. Make it the kind of place people want to go to because they feel loved and cared for. Be loving and friendly. Be considerate and on the lookout for new people. Be like Jesus! Your attitude, friendliness, compassion, and concern for others reflect the heart of Jesus. When a pastor leads from caring with a pastor's heart, these things naturally follow.

Scriptures to consider:

Jeremiah 3:14–15 (NKJV) *""Return, O backsliding children," says the Lord; "for I am married to you. I will take you, one from a city and two from a family, and I will bring you to Zion. And I will give you shepherds according to My heart, who will feed you with knowledge and understanding."*

1 Peter 5:2–4 (NKJV) *"Shepherd the flock of God which is among you, serving as overseers, not by compulsion but willingly, not for dishonest gain but eagerly; nor as being lords over those entrusted to you, but being examples to the flock; and when the Chief Shepherd appears, you will receive the crown of glory that does not fade away."*

_____

_____

_____

_____

_____

_____

_____

_____

_____

_____

_____

_____

_____

_____

_____

_____

12. A SERVANT'S HEART:
A pastor follows Jesus, committed to be the servant of all.

A servant's heart is a requirement for every pastor. Only God makes servants. The desire to serve others cannot be made up or faked. What you do, how you act, and the things you say reflect your character. True servants act, talk, and think like servants. The way of the Kingdom is not like the world. A pastor is never above serving in any way. Ask Jesus to give you a servant's heart and enlarge it day by day. Then, serve the Lord faithfully. Don't wait to be told to do something. Look out for things to do, people to serve, and then do them!

Pastoral ministry is service. Pastoral ministry is laying down your lives for others. Pastoral ministry is taking the place of a servant (spiritually), the servant of all. Pastoral ministry is walking in the footsteps of Jesus all the way to the cross. Jesus washed the disciples' feet and laid down his life for even those that hated Him. Look for ways to help the staff, the teams, your pastor, and the congregation. Even if, and especially when you have not been tasked with something to do, don't stand there idle but actively look around with spiritual eyes attentive to the practical and spiritual needs that are all around you. Respond to what you see. Some of the most beautiful agape love demonstrations are found in the most simple, regular acts of kindness. Men, we must endeavor to cultivate that fresh heart of a servant every day.

Scriptures to consider:

Matthew 23:11–12 (NKJV) "But he who is greatest among you shall be your servant. And whoever exalts himself will be humbled, and he who humbles himself will be exalted."

Mark 10:45 (NKJV) "For even the Son of Man did not come to be served, but to serve, and to give His life a ransom for many."

Matthew 23:11–12 (NKJV) "But he who is greatest among you shall be your servant. And whoever exalts himself will be humbled, and he who humbles himself will be exalted."

LEARNING AND GROWING IN PASTORAL MINISTRY

13. LIKE-MINDEDNESS WITH YOUR PASTOR:
A pastor is like-minded with his pastor.

More often than not, division begins because an assistant pastor doesn't have or has lost the essential like-mindedness with the pastor he serves alongside of in ministry. Like-mindedness is not conformity but rather a unity formed through relationship. Learning how to love through the challenges is needed in this new relationship with your pastor. Pray for your pastor, connect with your pastor and ask what his vision is for the particular ministry you have been entrusted with oversight. Take good notes from him, become a good listener, care for others how he would. Your role is not a stepping-stone to greater things. Serving Jesus is the greatest thing you can ever do! Remember that a healthy relationship with your pastor requires honesty, openness, and regular communication. If you're not like-minded with your pastor, talk to him, work it out, but don't cause division.

Scriptures to consider:

Amos 3:3 (NKJV) *"Can two walk together, unless they are agreed?"*

Philippians 2:1–2 (NKJV) *"Therefore if there is any consolation in Christ, if any comfort of love, if any fellowship of the Spirit, if any affection and mercy, fulfill my joy by being like-minded, having the same love, being of one accord, of one mind."*

Philippians 2:19–22 (NKJV) *"But I trust in the Lord Jesus to send Timothy to you shortly, that I also may be encouraged when I know your state. For I have no one like-minded, who will sincerely care for your state. For all seek their own, not the things which are of Christ Jesus. But you know his proven character, that as a son with his father he served with me in the gospel."*

_____

_____

_____

_____

_____

_____

_____

_____

_____

_____

_____

_____

_____

_____

_____

14. LOYALTY AND SUBMISSION:
A pastor is loyal, submissive, and committed to the Lord.

Loyalty to Jesus, your wife, other people, and your pastor is vital. Your pastor needs someone by his side who will support him, defend him, and be true to him and to the vision God has given him. Be a true friend and be loyal no matter what is happening. Stand by the man God has raised up to pastor the flock. Never are you required to overlook or excuse sin. Even in the worst of situations, point people to the Lord. Make unconditional love and fidelity your trademark.

There is one vision for the fellowship in which you serve. There are not two, not ten, not one hundred, but just one vision. Support your pastor's vision and help your ministry team to support it so that there is unity and peace among the flock. Lock shields together in unity! Pastors don't take personal advantage of difficult situations to further their own agendas or undermine leadership. The temptation to become an 'Absalom' is a familiar tool in the enemy's hands to destroy you and the ministry under your care. Faithful, supportive assistant pastors don't draw people's hearts after themselves. If their pastor seems off about something, they go to him and share the truth in love. Division is counterproductive to the cause of Christ.

Pastors don't steal sheep from other congregations, building a small kingdom for themselves on earth. They are careful to follow the model of Paul when he shared that he would not 'build on another man's foundation.' Division and disunity disrupt the peace and prosperity of the Holy Spirit.

Scriptures to consider:

Romans 13:1 (NKJV) *"Let every soul be subject to the governing authorities. For there is no authority except from God, and the authorities that exist are appointed by God."*

Romans 15:20 (NKJV) *"And so I have made it my aim to preach the gospel, not where Christ was named, lest I should build on another man's foundation,"*

Titus 3:1 (NKJV) *"Remind them to be subject to rulers and authorities, to obey, to be ready for every good work,"*

15. BE SUPPORTIVE AND HELPFUL:
A pastor follows the example of Aaron and Hur, holding up the arms of his pastor.

Your pastor needs help. Like Moses, his arms get weary. As long as Aaron and Hur held up Moses's arms, the battle went well for the nation of Israel. Moses needed help, and God provided men to come alongside of him. Together, with everyone doing their part, victory came! Victories in the battles of ministry happen the same way today. Stand by your pastor's side, loving him, helping him, supporting him, and praying for him. The last thing he needs is for you to hang on his arms, making the ministry harder than it already is.

Scriptures to consider:

Exodus 17:12–13 (NKJV) *"But Moses' hands became heavy; so they took a stone and put it under him, and he sat on it. And Aaron and Hur supported his hands, one on one side, and the other on the other side; and his hands were steady until the going down of the sun. So Joshua defeated Amalek and his people with the edge of the sword."*

Hebrews 13:17 (NKJV) *"Obey those who rule over you, and be submissive, for they watch out for your souls, as those who must give account. Let them do so with joy and not with grief, for that would be unprofitable for you."*

_____

_____

_____

_____

_____

_____

16. CONFIDENTIALITY AND THE CONFIDENCE OF OTHERS:
Confidentiality is an essential component of his trustworthiness in ministry.

A pastor understands that keeping things in confidence is essential. When you breach confidentiality, you lose that important place of trust and authority in someone's life. You must be trustworthy with the information you see, hear, and with what people share with you. Confidentiality speaks of the 'confidence' that someone puts in you to trust you with their life. Confidentiality protects the rights and dignity of others. Its opposite counterpart: gossip destroys people, including you. Remember, some things need to be reported immediately, like any abuse or accusations related to a child's safety, etc. When in doubt, go directly to your pastor. He will help. However, most things that are shared in confidence need to remain protected so that people are not needlessly hurt by sinful discussions.

Scriptures to consider:

Luke 12:2–3 (NKJV) *"For there is nothing covered that will not be revealed, nor hidden that will not be known. Therefore whatever you have spoken in the dark will be heard in the light, and what you have spoken in the ear in inner rooms will be proclaimed on the housetops."*

Proverbs 11:13 (NKJV) *"A talebearer reveals secrets, But he who is of a faithful spirit conceals a matter."*

Proverbs 18:19 (NKJV) *"A brother offended is harder to win than a strong city, And contentions are like the bars of a castle."*

_____

_____

_____

_____

_____

_____

_____

_____

_____

_____

_____

_____

_____

_____

_____

_____

_____

_____

_____

_____

17. 24/7 MINISTRY:
A pastor is a pastor 24/7.

The ministry of the pastor involves a 24/7 commitment. This commitment means that a pastor is ready to serve whenever ministry needs are present. Pastoral care is not a 9 to 5 job. Actually, it's not a job at all but God's calling upon your life! You can't schedule when pain enters into a family's life; neither can you simply clock out and no longer care. Some seasons of pastoral ministry are more challenging than others, but a pastor is ready whenever ministry is needed. You're always a pastor everywhere and anywhere you are.

If you are a clock watcher, then pastoral ministry is simply not for you. If you are the type of person that likes to 'learn the system' and offer to God and your church the least amount of effort doing the bare minimum, pastoral ministry is not for you. Ministry is labor, a labor of love. While it is tremendously rewarding, it can also be tremendously demanding.

Scriptures to consider:

Mark 4:38–39 (NKJV) *"But He was in the stern, asleep on a pillow. And they awoke Him and said to Him, "Teacher, do You not care that we are perishing?" Then He arose and rebuked the wind, and said to the sea, "Peace, be still!" And the wind ceased and there was a great calm."*

Mark 6:30–34 (NKJV) *Then the apostles gathered to Jesus and told Him all things, both what they had done and what they had taught. And He said to them, "Come aside by yourselves to a deserted place and rest a while." For there were many coming and going, and they did not even have time to eat. So they depart-ed to a deserted place in the boat by themselves. But the multitudes saw them departing, and many knew Him and ran there on foot from all the cities. They arrived before them and came together to Him. And Jesus, when He came out, saw a great multitude and was moved with compassion for them, because they were like sheep not having a shepherd. So He began to teach them many things.*

_____

_____

_____

18. KNOW THE STATE OF YOUR FLOCKS:
A pastor knows the state of God's flock.

A pastor should care, and part of caring is knowing how the people are doing. Effective and fruitful pastoral ministry is highly relational. When caring for His flock, a pastor is not merely responding to needs, but he is regularly checking in, wanting to know how people are doing, and ever gaining new knowledge about the care and concern for the flock of God. A pastor knows the importance of following up. He uses technology to communicate well.

Scriptures to consider:

Proverbs 27:23 (NKJV) *"Be diligent to know the state of your flocks, And attend to your herds;"*

Ezekiel 34:1–2 (NKJV) *"And the word of the Lord came to me, saying, "Son of man, prophesy against the shepherds of Israel, prophesy and say to them, 'Thus says the Lord God to the shepherds: "Woe to the shepherds of Israel who feed themselves! Should not the shepherds feed the flocks?"*

Acts 20:28 (NKJV) *"Therefore take heed to yourselves and to all the flock, among which the Holy Spirit has made you overseers, to shepherd the church of God which He purchased with His own blood."*

_____

_____

_____

_____

_____

_____

19. MAKE DISCIPLES:
A pastor enjoys and regularly makes disciples of Jesus.

The Great Commission given by Jesus is to make disciples. A pastor's role is to equip the saints for the work of the ministry. You're either making disciples, or you're not. Men will often join a church staff and quickly forget that they are there to build up the Body of Christ. It's good to look at every situation as a 'discipleship moment'. You will either be building up a disciple (follower of Christ) or neglecting them. You have the joy and privilege of raising up new servants, leaders, and disciples of Christ. Whether it's by developing ministry teams or raising up a 'Timothy', disciple-making is your heavenly mandate.

Scriptures to consider:

Matthew 28:19–20 (NKJV) *"Go therefore and make disciples of all the nations, baptizing them in the name of the Father and of the Son and of the Holy Spirit, teaching them to observe all things that I have commanded you; and lo, I am with you always, even to the end of the age." Amen."*

Ephesians 4:11–16 (NKJV) *"And He Himself gave some to be apostles, some prophets, some evangelists, and some pastors and teachers, for the equipping of the saints for the work of ministry, for the edifying of the body of Christ, till we all come to the unity of the faith and of the knowledge of the Son of God, to a perfect man, to the measure of the stature of the fullness of Christ; that we should no longer be children, tossed to and fro and carried about with every wind of doctrine, by the trickery of men, in the cunning craftiness of deceitful plotting, but, speaking the truth in love, may grow up in all things into Him who is the head—Christ—from whom the whole body, joined and knit together by what every joint supplies, according to the effective working by which every part does its share, causes growth of the body for the edifying of itself in love."*

20. MAINTAINS AN ATMOSPHERE OF LOVE AND GRACE:

A pastor regularly loves and encourages to help maintain an atmosphere of love.

We are given opportunities to love and serve people all the time. It's vital that you choose to step into those openings with love and grace. As a pastor, you can create a loving environment in the ministry by encouraging others, praying for them, checking in on them, and lovingly serving them by grace. As you are serving God's people, don't forget the visitors, the strangers, other servants, and a whole host of people God will bring your way. Help the ladies with their boxes, the moms with their kids, and anyone the Lord would lead you to help, serve, and express His love and grace to them. Don't stand around ignoring the opportunities to spread the love of Jesus throughout the ministry. If you are harsh and impatient, you are not reflecting the heart of Jesus and don't belong in the ministry.

Scriptures to consider:

Matthew 5:9 (NKJV) *"Blessed are the peacemakers, For they shall be called sons of God."*

Colossians 3:13–15 (NKJV) *"Bearing with one another, and forgiving one another, if anyone has a complaint against another; even as Christ forgave you, so you also must do. But above all these things put on love, which is the bond of perfection. And let the peace of God rule in your hearts, to which also you were called in one body; and be thankful."*

_____

_____

_____

_____

_____

_____

21. PLAYER / COACH:
A pastor serves alongside those serving Jesus.

There are many practical and relevant ways to describe a pastor's leadership and oversight. A great picture is one of a Coach helping others fulfill their God-given callings while at the same time being a player fulfilling your own. You're both on the field directing and in the game yourself. In other words, like Jesus taught us, we don't serve in a hierarchy type of system as the world does. You don't climb the ladder. Jesus taught us that the way up is actually down. We never arrive at a place where we don't 'have to serve' any longer. Don't underestimate the power of your daily example in both overseeing and serving the Lord.

Scriptures to consider:

Mark 6:41–42 (NKJV) *"And when He had taken the five loaves and the two fish, He looked up to heaven, blessed and broke the loaves, and gave them to His disciples to set before them; and the two fish He divided among them all. So they all ate and were filled."*

Mark 9:35 (NKJV) *And He sat down, called the twelve, and said to them, "If anyone desires to be first, he shall be last of all and servant of all."*

1 Peter 4:10–11 (NKJV) *"As each one has received a gift, minister it to one another, as good stewards of the manifold grace of God. If anyone speaks, let him speak as the oracles of God. If anyone ministers, let him do it as with the ability which God supplies, that in all things God may be glorified through Jesus Christ, to whom belong the glory and the dominion forever and ever. Amen."*

_____

_____

_____

_____

_____

_____

22. BE AN EXAMPLE:
A pastor is a biblical example to others.

Don't underestimate the immense power of your example to others. The Bible instructs us to be an example in word, deed, and life. Every area of a pastor's life is an example to others. What you say, how you respond, and how you react are important in your pastoral ministry. You must be careful of coarse jesting and harmful goofing around. This is not to say you won't be happy and joke around, but rather you must be careful to walk in the Spirit, not fulfilling the lust of your flesh. People are always watching you looking for ways to improve their spiritual lives. You are either a good example or a bad example, but you are an example for others to follow in their relationship with Jesus.

Scriptures to consider:

1 Samuel 16:7 (NKJV) *"But the Lord said to Samuel, "Do not look at his appearance or at his physical stature, because I have refused him. For the Lord does not see as man sees; for man looks at the outward appearance, but the Lord looks at the heart."*

Ephesians 5:3–4 (NKJV) *"But fornication and all uncleanness or covetousness, let it not even be named among you, as is fitting for saints; neither filthiness, nor foolish talking, nor coarse jesting, which are not fitting, but rather giving of thanks."*

1 Timothy 4:12–13 (NKJV) *"Let no one despise your youth, but be an example to the believers in word, in conduct, in love, in spirit, in faith, in purity. Till I come, give attention to reading, to exhortation, to doctrine."*

Titus 2:6–8 (NKJV) *"Likewise, exhort the young men to be sober-minded, in all things showing yourself to be a pattern of good works; in doctrine showing integrity, reverence, incorruptibility, sound speech that cannot be condemned, that one who is an opponent may be ashamed, having nothing evil to say of you."*

_____

_____

_____

_____

23. PASTOR TO EACH OTHER:
A pastor serves his co-workers and co-laborers.

A pastor is a man representing Jesus to everyone. We are co-laborers serving one another regardless of our title. When a man joins a ministry team as a pastor, he can easily forget his role to serve everyone, including those he 'works' alongside. It is a privilege to pastor one another as you are a vital part of one another's lives. A pastor is a pastor to the receptionist, fellow pastors, co-workers, their families, and truly, anyone and everyone. Ministry is relational, but it's spiritual first. There will be times when a pastor must speak the truth in love to even his closest of friends. More often than not, you will have the joy of speaking truth, encouragement, and hope into each other's lives. Never forget, we are to pastor everyone as the Lord leads us.

Scripture to consider:

Hebrews 10:24–25 (NKJV) *"And let us consider one another in order to stir up love and good works, not forsaking the assembling of ourselves together, as is the manner of some, but exhorting one another, and so much the more as you see the Day approaching."*

_____

_____

_____

_____

_____

_____

_____

24. HELPING FELLOW PASTORS:
A pastor 'pastors' his fellow pastors.

" We" is always the language of unity and ministry. None of us serve alone. One role you will have is to help your fellow pastors grow in grace as they exercise their calling, commitments, and steady obedience. There is a need to pastor your fellow pastors through the good times and through the challenging times. It will not please God nor help the Church to overlook blatant sin or approve of behavior unbecoming of a pastor. Instead, what pleases God is for a pastor to remember that he is to pastor everyone, all the time, including those who pastor and shepherd the flock alongside of him.

Scriptures to consider:

Ecclesiastes 4:9–10 (NKJV) "Two are better than one, Because they have a good reward for their labor. For if they fall, one will lift up his companion. But woe to him who is alone when he falls, For he has no one to help him up."

Galatians 6:2–3 (NKJV) "Bear one another's burdens, and so fulfill the law of Christ. For if anyone thinks himself to be something, when he is nothing, he deceives himself."

25. USING TIME WISELY:
A pastor is known for his punctuality and faithfulness.

A pastor is known for his punctuality and using his spare time for the glory of God. Being on time means being early, ready to start the day in ministry unhindered. Being late is not becoming of a pastor as it sends mixed messages of laziness, apathy, and that others' time is not valuable to you. Be early to everything, ready to serve the Lord and His people. How you use your spare time, both in the office and at home, will determine your ministry's effectiveness. You will undoubtedly have times where there seems to be "nothing" to do at the office. In any sized church, there is NEVER 'nothing' to do. There are always people to see, people to reach out to, people to love, people to care for. There are countless practical things to take care of like; cleaning, fixing, and caring for the facilities. Laziness and wasting time (goofing off) are not becoming of a pastor and rob you of your own personal growth in the ministry.

Scriptures to consider:

Ecclesiastes 3:1 (NKJV) "To everything there is a season, A time for every purpose under heaven:"

Ephesians 5:15–16 (NKJV) "See then that you walk circumspectly, not as fools but as wise, redeeming the time, because the days are evil."

1 Corinthians 14:40 (NKJV) "Let all things be done decently and in order."

LEARNING AND GROWING IN PASTORAL MINISTRY

26. USING YOUR OFFICE TIME WISELY:
A pastor uses his office strategically, knowing people are most important.

While most pastors will have an office, much of the ministry doesn't take place there. It takes place with people. The most important time around a building is when people are on the property! Don't hide in your office from people. Be among the flock serving them, loving them, caring for them. A pastor's role is to care for the flock's practical and spiritual day-to-day needs. It is not to stay in his office all day studying. You are a part of a dynamic team serving and ministering to people, not holed up in an office reading and studying, and otherwise not engaged with the people you're here to serve.

While studying is important, your role as a pastor is to study the congregation, looking for ways to serve. Sitting isolated in your office behind a computer is not helping you grow in ministering to the flock. Look for ways to be 'among' the flock of God and serve them well. It is a bad habit to be in your office and not among the people. A pastor will be a good steward of his time.

Scriptures to consider:

Romans 12:9–13 (NKJV) "Let love be without hypocrisy. Abhor what is evil. Cling to what is good. Be kindly affectionate to one another with brotherly love, in honor giving preference to one another; not lagging in diligence, fervent in spirit, serving the Lord; rejoicing in hope, patient in tribulation, continuing steadfastly in prayer; distributing to the needs of the saints, given to hospitality."

2 Timothy 2:14–15 (NKJV) "Remind them of these things, charging them before the Lord not to strive about words to no profit, to the ruin of the hearers. Be diligent to present yourself approved to God, a worker who does not need to be ashamed, rightly dividing the word of truth."

USING FREEDOM FOR THE GLORY OF GOD:
A pastor uses His freedoms to honor God.

Because a pastor operates in a working atmosphere of a lot of freedom, he must wisely choose to use those freedoms for others and not himself. A pastor will face daily choices of how to use his time balanced with his freedom. How you make these choices will determine your spiritual effectiveness. Will you take care of personal business instead of ministry? Will you take an extended lunchtime to go shopping for your home? Using your time unwisely leads you into the realm of dishonesty and deceit, two things not to be named among pastors. Remember, just because you can, doesn't mean you should. Your freedom is not a cloak for vice but a tool to use in serving God and His people!

Scriptures to consider:

Galatians 5:13 (NKJV) *"For you, brethren, have been called to liberty; only do not use liberty as an opportunity for the flesh, but through love serve one another."*

Philippians 2:4 (NKJV) *"Let each of you look out not only for his own interests, but also for the interests of others."*

1 Peter 2:15–16 (NKJV) *"For this is the will of God, that by doing good you may put to silence the ignorance of foolish men—as free, yet not using liberty as a cloak for vice, but as bondservants of God."*

COMMUNICATION:
A pastor is regularly a clear communicator.

In light of the Gospel, honoring Jesus, helping others, proclaiming the Good News, and a whole host of glorious blessings the Church brings to the world, the essential "business" (for lack of a better term) of the Church is communication. The better we communicate both verbally and nonverbally, the more people are saved, loved, cared for, encouraged, strengthened, and helped. How we communicate is important as well. We must pray for the ability to listen and communicate well. As we walk in the Spirit, He will help us with our tone of voice, body language, and everything else that helps connect with a person in love. It's vital that you communicate and communicate well.

Scriptures to consider:

Nehemiah 8:1–2 (NKJV) *"Now all the people gathered together as one man in the open square that was in front of the Water Gate; and they told Ezra the scribe to bring the Book of the Law of Moses, which the Lord had commanded Israel. So Ezra the priest brought the Law before the assembly of men and women and all who could hear with understanding on the first day of the seventh month."*

Romans 14:19 (NKJV) *"Therefore let us pursue the things which make for peace and the things by which one may edify another."*

_____

_____

_____

_____

_____

_____

29. **COMMUNICATION WITH YOUR PASTOR:**
A pastor communicates frequently and clearly with the Lead / Senior Pastor.

You cannot over-communicate with your Lead/Senior pastor. You are the eyes and the ears of the ministry. He needs to know what you know so together; you can oversee the fellowship of God without confusion, giving no room for the enemy to take advantage of you. You are responsible for being another set of eyes and the ears of the ministry. "We" is the language of ministry and communicating with your pastor will assure the unity of the Spirit in the bond of peace.

Scriptures to consider:

Romans 14:19 (NKJV) *"Therefore let us pursue the things which make for peace and the things by which one may edify another."*

1 John 1:6–7 (NKJV) *"If we say that we have fellowship with Him, and walk in darkness, we lie and do not practice the truth. But if we walk in the light as He is in the light, we have fellowship with one another, and the blood of Jesus Christ His Son cleanses us from all sin."*

30. FOLLOWING UP, THROUGH, AND ON:
A pastor knows the importance of following up.

As a pastor, you're being invited into someone's life. There is a process of relationship that begins and continues far beyond the event that started it. Never forget that ministry continues on past the "event" or crisis. Without proper follow-up, people are neglected. Part of communicating well is closing any gaps of people waiting to hear back from us. I call this the importance of Following Up (within 24 hours), Following Through (within days, weeks), and Following On (until the rapture). Using your reminder apps, calendar, and other tools will help you serve God's people well until He returns.

Scripture to consider:

Hebrews 10:23–25 (NKJV) "Let us hold fast the confession of our hope without wavering, for He who promised is faithful. And let us consider one another in order to stir up love and good works, not forsaking the assembling of ourselves together, as is the manner of some, but exhorting one another, and so much the more as you see the Day approaching."

_____

_____

_____

_____

_____

_____

_____

_____

31. PHONE CALLS, EMAIL, TEXT MESSAGES AND SOCIAL MEDIA:

A pastor uses technology to communicate well.

A pastor will honor God through his faithful communication. Technology has made it more convenient than ever to communicate. However, because so much information comes to a pastor every day, it's also easier not to respond to others at all. It's expected that you return phone calls (within 24 hours), emails (within a day), text messages (within 12 hours), and social media (regularly). Today, people communicate differently, so adapt your thinking to ensure no one is waiting on you.

Scripture to consider:

Philippians 2:4 (NKJV) *"Let each of you look out not only for his own interests, but also for the interests of others."*

_____

_____

_____

_____

_____

_____

_____

_____

_____

_____

32. REACHING OUT:
A pastor is always reaching out.

Jesus promised to make us fishers of men. As pastors, that's exactly what we are. Just as fish cannot be caught without throwing a hook or a net into the water, much of ministry doesn't occur without a pastor reaching out regularly and checking in on his leaders, those who serve with him, the flock, his co-workers, etc. This proactive part of ministry can be the most fun as you have the opportunity to be used in a person's life led directly by the Holy Spirit. Regular communication affirms your care in a person's life and is often greatly appreciated by those you are lovingly serving.

Scriptures to consider:

Ezekiel 34:12 (NKJV) *"As a shepherd seeks out his flock on the day he is among his scattered sheep, so will I seek out My sheep and deliver them from all the places where they were scattered on a cloudy and dark day."*

1 Thessalonians 5:11 (NKJV) *"Therefore comfort each other and edify one another, just as you also are doing."*

_____

_____

_____

_____

_____

_____

_____

_____

33. CARRYING YOUR BIBLE AND A NOTEPAD:
A pastor takes his physical Bible with him everywhere.

A pastor's primary tools are the Bible and prayer. It's essential that a pastor has his Bible with him at all times so that people can see the authority he walks in is not his own but from God and His Word. Using an iPhone or iPad is no substitute for carrying and using your Bible. Carrying a notepad allows you to jot down things you see, or hear, and remind yourself of people or situations to follow up with. With so much going on, it's easy to forget things. Write them down to follow up as soon as possible.

Scripture to consider:

2 Timothy 3:16–17 (NKJV) *"All Scripture is given by inspiration of God, and is profitable for doctrine, for reproof, for correction, for instruction in righteousness, that the man of God may be complete, thoroughly equipped for every good work."*

_____

_____

_____

_____

_____

_____

_____

_____

_____

FIFTEEN MINUTES BEFORE AND AFTER SERVICES:
A pastor is in the sanctuary praying, greeting, and encouraging.

A pastor's role is to be among the people, and he needs to be in the sanctuary greeting, praying, ministering, and serving the flock during these critical times. Don't underestimate the value of a two-minute conversation with someone that validates your love for them and encourages them to feel loved and appreciated. Many times, this short connection will lead to deeper ministry opportunities. It's during the regular Church service times that have the largest amount of precious people on the property at one time. Some of the most important ministry time is 15 minutes before the service starts and 15 minutes after the service concludes. A pastor uses the first 15 minutes before a service in the sanctuary to greet, encourage, welcome and pray with those who are waiting for the service to start. A pastor uses the final 15 minutes after a service in the sanctuary to check in on and pray for those who are processing all that they have received.

Scriptures to consider:

Matthew 14:14 (NKJV) "And when Jesus went out He saw a great multitude; and He was moved with compassion for them, and healed their sick."

Acts 20:28 (NKJV) "Therefore take heed to yourselves and to all the flock, among which the Holy Spirit has made you overseers, to shepherd the church of God which He purchased with His own blood."

1 Peter 5:2 (NKJV) "Shepherd the flock of God which is among you, serving as overseers, not by compulsion but willingly, not for dishonest gain but eagerly;"

_____

_____

_____

_____

_____

35. CHURCH BUSINESS AT SERVICES:
A pastor handles 'church business' at appropriate times.

As a pastor it's important to train and disciple leaders to deal with 'church business' issues after engaging and caring for the needs of the people. It's easy to get caught up in administrative church business during service times, but it's always the people that suffer by not being cared for. In order to avoid neglecting the needs of the flock at the larger gatherings the people need to get our full attention and church business can wait until a more appropriate time.

Scripture to consider:

Ephesians 5:15–17 (NKJV) *"See then that you walk circumspectly, not as fools but as wise, redeeming the time, because the days are evil. Therefore do not be unwise, but understand what the will of the Lord is."*

_____

_____

_____

_____

_____

_____

_____

_____

_____

_____

36. BIBLICAL DISCIPLESHIP:
A pastor provides biblical discipleship to the flock.

A large part of a pastor's time will be investing the Word of God into the lives of those who ask for help. Sometimes this is called counseling, but it's better termed "Biblical Discipleship." The ultimate goal is their progressive sanctification. As a pastor, you are not a professional counselor, but rather someone used by God to help others get on the right track with their lives in Christ. This type of discipleship often involves scheduling appointments with couples, and singles, to listen to their issues and respond with the Word of God. They do not need *your* opinion, but they do need you to pray with them and point them to the Word of God for their situation.

Scriptures to consider:

Proverbs 3:5–6 (NKJV) *"Trust in the Lord with all your heart, And lean not on your own understanding; In all your ways acknowledge Him, And He shall direct your paths."*

2 Timothy 2:24–26 (NKJV) *"And a servant of the Lord must not quarrel but be gentle to all, able to teach, patient, in humility correcting those who are in opposition, if God perhaps will grant them repentance, so that they may know the truth, and that they may come to their senses and escape the snare of the devil, having been taken captive by him to do his will."*

Titus 1:9 (NKJV) *"Holding fast the faithful word as he has been taught, that he may be able, by sound doctrine, both to exhort and convict those who contradict."*

_____

_____

_____

_____

_____

_____

LEARNING AND GROWING IN PASTORAL MINISTRY

37. INVITING YOURSELF INTO LIVES:
A pastor invites himself graciously into the lives of others.

There are so many needs within the Church that it can be very overwhelming. However, serving people is not merely a reaction to others asking for help. As we walk in the Spirit, we will often be led to invite ourselves into the lives of others, asking for their permission to share a word, visit them, making ourselves available. Being ready and willing to ask, "how can I serve you" is one of the most fulfilling parts of ministry. If you only react, you're setting yourself up to be discouraged, disappointed, and overwhelmed.

Scriptures to consider:

Luke 19:5 (NKJV)And when Jesus came to the place, He looked up and saw him, and said to him, "Zacchaeus, make haste and come down, for today I must stay at your house."

John 4:4 (NKJV) "But He needed to go through Samaria."

_____

_____

_____

_____

_____

_____

_____

_____

38. WALK-INS:
A pastor is ready to serve anyone that walks in the door.

On occasion, men and women will show up unannounced and unexpected to the property wanting help. A pastor will respond in love to walk-ins, investing the needed time at the moment to serve their needs using prayer and the Bible.

Scripture to consider:

1 Peter 4:9–11 (NKJV) *"Be hospitable to one another without grumbling. As each one has received a gift, minister it to one another, as good stewards of the manifold grace of God. If anyone speaks, let him speak as the oracles of God. If anyone ministers, let him do it as with the ability which God supplies, that in all things God may be glorified through Jesus Christ, to whom belong the glory and the dominion forever and ever. Amen."*

39. BENEVOLENCE:
A pastor helps distribute to the needs of the needy.

A pastor is to tend to the practical needs of those that are hurting.
A pastor will help distribute through the benevolence of the church or his
own resources to help the hurting.

Scripture to consider:

Galatians 2:9–10 (NKJV) *"And when James, Cephas, and John, who seemed to
be pillars, perceived the grace that had been given to me, they gave me and
Barnabas the right hand of fellowship, that we should go to the Gentiles and they
to the circumcised. They desired only that we should remember the poor, the very
thing which I also was eager to do."*

_____

_____

_____

_____

_____

_____

_____

_____

_____

_____

_____

LEARNING AND GROWING IN PASTORAL MINISTRY

40. HOSPITAL AND HOME VISITS:
A pastor will visit the sick in their homes or hospitals.

When someone is sick, dying, or homebound, it's the pastor's privilege to visit them and encourage them with his presence, the Word of God, and prayer. These visits are by far one of the most joyful honors to be alongside someone in their loneliness or sickness. Whether you are invited or you ask to come over, do so with the joy and encouragement of the Holy Spirit.

Scripture to consider:

James 5:14–15 (NKJV) *"Is anyone among you sick? Let him call for the elders of the church, and let them pray over him, anointing him with oil in the name of the Lord. And the prayer of faith will save the sick, and the Lord will raise him up. And if he has committed sins, he will be forgiven."*

_____

_____

_____

_____

_____

_____

_____

_____

_____

_____

41. BABY DEDICATIONS:
A pastor helps families dedicate their children to God.

Baby dedications are a wonderful step for a family on their journey of discipling their children. A pastor is involved in praying, encouraging, and helping a mom and dad know what the Bible says about raising their children in the ways of the Lord.

Scripture to consider:

Luke 2:22–24 (NKJV) "Now when the days of her purification according to the law of Moses were completed, they brought Him to Jerusalem to present Him to the Lord (as it is written in the law of the Lord, "Every male who opens the womb shall be called holy to the Lord"), and to offer a sacrifice according to what is said in the law of the Lord, "A pair of turtledoves or two young pigeons."

_____

_____

_____

_____

_____

_____

_____

_____

_____

_____

42. PRE-MARITAL DISCIPLESHIP:
A pastor helps a couple prepare for marriage biblically.

We want to do everything possible to help prepare a couple for their lifelong covenant of marriage together. Using the Bible and prayer, along with our pre-marital resources, we will help disciple a couple through the key elements of marriage. Pre-marital discipleship usually takes six months or longer.

Scriptures to consider:

Titus 1:9 (NKJV) *"Holding fast the faithful word as he has been taught, that he may be able, by sound doctrine, both to exhort and convict those who contradict."*

Hebrews 13:4 (NKJV) *"Marriage is honorable among all, and the bed undefiled; but fornicators and adulterers God will judge."*

_____

_____

_____

_____

_____

_____

_____

_____

_____

43. WEDDINGS:

A pastor will officiate weddings as a representative of God and of his local church.

Weddings are always a glorious event. As a part of our pastoral ministry, the Lord allows us to represent Him as the officiant of one man and one woman, becoming one in the sight of God and man. Sometimes this happens at the church building, and other times, it occurs at an outside venue. Officiating a wedding is a joyful honor.

Scriptures to consider:

Mark 10:6–9 (NKJV) *"But from the beginning of the creation, God 'made them male and female.' 'For this reason a man shall leave his father and mother and be joined to his wife, and the two shall become one flesh'; so then they are no longer two, but one flesh. Therefore what God has joined together, let not man separate."*

Hebrews 13:4 (NKJV) *"Marriage is honorable among all, and the bed undefiled; but fornicators and adulterers God will judge."*

_____

_____

_____

_____

_____

_____

_____

_____

_____

LEARNING AND GROWING IN PASTORAL MINISTRY

44. FUNERALS:
A pastor will officiate funerals serving the survivors of death.

It is often a sad and solemn time when a person, a loved one, dies. A pastor will be used by God to bring comfort, encouragement, and hope to those who have survived the death of someone they cared for and loved. He will walk with them through this difficult time, often as an officiant of the memorial and graveside services. It is a high honor to care for a family spiritually during this time.

Scriptures to consider:

Romans 12:14–15 (NKJV) *"Bless those who persecute you; bless and do not curse. Rejoice with those who rejoice, and weep with those who weep."*

2 Corinthians 1:3–5 (NKJV) *"Blessed be the God and Father of our Lord Jesus Christ, the Father of mercies and God of all comfort, who comforts us in all our tribulation, that we may be able to comfort those who are in any trouble, with the comfort with which we ourselves are comforted by God. For as the sufferings of Christ abound in us, so our consolation also abounds through Christ."*

_____

_____

_____

_____

_____

_____

_____

_____

LEARNING AND GROWING IN PASTORAL MINISTRY

45. INVITATIONS, NOT INTERRUPTIONS:
A pastor realizes that God brings the people into his life.

Ministry is not a series of never-ending tasks. Ministry is all about souls! It's easy to become frustrated when there are so many things to do, people to see, so much sadness and gladness, brokenness, and pain. This frustration can lead to seeing ministry to people as an interruption instead of a God-ordained invitation into His ministry. Be careful not to despise the ministry of the Lord and choose to see seeming interruptions as invitations into ministry with Jesus.

Scripture to consider:

Luke 8:45–48 (NKJV) *"And Jesus said, "Who touched Me?" When all denied it, Peter and those with him said, "Master, the multitudes throng and press You, and You say, 'Who touched Me?'" But Jesus said, "Somebody touched Me, for I perceived power going out from Me." Now when the woman saw that she was not hidden, she came trembling; and falling down before Him, she declared to Him in the presence of all the people the reason she had touched Him and how she was healed immediately. And He said to her, "Daughter, be of good cheer; your faith has made you well. Go in peace."*

_____

_____

_____

_____

_____

_____

_____

_____

EVANGELISM IS THE HEART.

WIN:
Mark 16:15 "And He said to them, "Go into all the world and preach the gospel to every creature.""

DISCIPLE:
Matthew 28:19 "Go therefore and make disciples of all the nations, baptizing them in the name of the Father and of the Son and of the Holy Spirit"

SEND:
Acts 1:8 "But you shall receive power when the Holy Spirit has come upon you; and you shall be witnesses to Me in Jerusalem, and in all Judea and Samaria, and to the end of the earth."

OUR JERUSALEM: Aurora
OUR JUDEA: Denver Metro Area & surrounding communities
OUR SAMARIA: Colorado & the U.S.
OUR ENDS OF THE EARTH: The globe

"WE WILL DO ANYTHING SHORT OF SIN TO REACH PEOPLE WHO DON'T KNOW JESUS."

STATEMENT OF FAITH

Calvary Chapel Churches have been formed as a fellowship of believers under the Lordship of Jesus Christ. Our supreme desire is know Christ and be conformed to His image by the power of the Holy Spirit.
We are not a denominational church, nor are we opposed to denominations as such; only to their over-emphasis of the doctrinal differences that have led to the division of the Body of Christ.
We believe the only true basis of Christian fellowship is Christ's (Agape) love, which is greater than differences we possess, and without which we have no right to claim ourselves Christians.

DOCTRINAL BELIEFS

#1
We believe in what is termed "The Apostles' Creed" as embodying all the fundamental doctrines of orthodox evangelical Christianity.

#2
We believe there is one living and true God, eternally existing in three persons; the Father, the Son, and the Holy Spirit, equal in power and glory; that this triune God created all, upholds all, and governs all.

#3
We believe in God, the Father, an infinite, personal Spirit, perfect in holiness, wisdom, power, and love; that He concerns Himself mercifully in the affairs of men; that He hears and answers prayer; and that He saves from sin and death all who come to Him through Jesus Christ.

#4
We believe in Jesus Christ, God's only begotten Son, conceived by the Holy Spirit. We believe in His virgin birth, sinless life, miracles, and teachings; His substitutionary atoning death; bodily resurrection; ascension into heaven; perpetual intercession for His people; and personal, visible return to earth. We believe that He is one and the same as God. He was fully human and fully God.

#5
We believe in the Holy Spirit, who came forth from the Father and Son to convict the world of sin, righteousness, and judgment and to regenerate, sanctify, and empower in ministry all who believe in Christ. We believe the Holy Spirit indwells every believer in Jesus Christ and that He is an abiding Helper, Teacher, and Guide. We believe that Jesus Christ baptizes the seeking believer with the Holy Spirit and power for service, either at the time of or subsequent to regeneration, which is a separate work from the indwelling Spirit for salvation. We believe in the present ministry of the Holy Spirit and in the exercise of all biblical gifts of the Spirit as reflected through the fruit of that same Spirit.

#6
We believe that all the Scriptures of the Old and New Testaments are the Word of God, fully inspired and without error in the original manuscripts, and that they are the infallible rule of faith and practice.

#7

We believe all people are by nature separated from God and responsible for their own sin, but that salvation, redemption, and forgiveness are freely offered to all by the grace of our Lord Jesus Christ. When a person repents of sin and accepts Jesus Christ as his/her personal Lord and Savior, trusting Him to save, that person is immediately born again and sealed by the Holy Spirit, all of his/her sins are forgiven, and that person becomes a child of God, destined to spend eternity with the Lord.

#8

We await the pre-tribulation rapture of the church, and we believe in the literal Second Coming of Christ with His saints to rule the earth, which will be personal and visible. This motivates us to holy living, heartfelt worship, committed service, diligent study of God's Word, regular fellowship, participation in adult baptism by immersion and Holy Communion.

#9

We are neither Five-Point Calvinists, nor are we Arminians. We adhere firmly to the biblical teaching of God's sovereignty and man's responsibility. We avoid any theological systems of belief that go beyond the written Word and thereby divide the body of Christ.

#10

We do not believe in "positive confession" (the faith movement belief that God can be commanded to heal or work miracles according to man's will); human prophecy that supersedes the Scriptures; the incorporation of humanistic and secular psychology into biblical teaching; the overemphasis of spiritual gifts and experiential signs and wonders to the exclusion of biblical teaching; or that true Christians can be demon-possessed.

#11

We believe in the universal Church, in the living spiritual body, of which Christ is the head and all regenerated persons are members.

#12

We believe the Lord Jesus Christ committed two ordinances to the Church: 1) baptism, and 2) the Lord's Supper. We believe in baptism by immersion and communion, both of which are open to all believers in Jesus Christ.

#13

We believe in the laying on of hands for the sending out of pastors and missionaries, and in conjunction with the anointing of oil by the elders for the healing of the sick.

PRACTICAL BELIEFS

#1
We believe the only true basis of Christian fellowship is Christ's (agape) love, which is greater than differences we possess, and without which we have no right to claim ourselves Christians.

#2
We believe worship of God should be spiritual; therefore, we remain flexible and yielded to the leading of the Holy Spirit to direct our worship.

#3
We believe worship of God should be inspirational; therefore, we give great place to music in our worship.

#4
We believe worship of God should be intelligent; therefore, our services are designed with great emphasis upon the teaching of the Word of God that He might instruct us on how He should be worshiped. We seek to teach the Word of God in such a way that its message can be applied to the individual's life, leading that person to a greater maturity in Christ. We teach both expositionally and topically.

#5
We believe that the Bible clearly delineates that spiritual gifts are for the edification of the body and that they are to be exercised in love. We believe that love is more important than the most spectacular gifts, and without love, all exercise of spiritual gifts is worthless. In our services, we focus on a personal relationship with God through worship, prayer, and the teaching of the Word of God. We do not practice speaking in tongues during worship or while a Bible study is in progress because we do not believe that the Holy Spirit would interrupt Himself. God is not the author of confusion. These gifts are encouraged in more intimate settings, e.g. personal prayer times, and afterglow services where their benefit can accomplish the purpose for which they have been given - the edification of the body of Christ.

#6
We believe that the church government should be simplistic rather than a complex bureaucracy, and we depend on the Holy Spirit to lead, rather than on fleshly promotion.

#7
We believe worship of God should be fruitful; therefore, we look for His love in our lives as the supreme manifestation that we have been truly worshiping Him.

PHILOSOPHY OF MINISTRY

Calvary Chapel Churches have been a tremendous example of how God honors His Word. Calvary Church is a fellowship planted in Aurora to bring glory and honor to His name. Highlighted below are fifteen key biblical truths that serve to guide our fellowship and ministry here. It is on these sound biblical foundations that Calvary Church is firmly planted.

15 BIBLICAL TRUTHS

#1 | "THE MINISTRY BELONGS TO THE LORD" - ZECHARIAH 4:6
"Not by might nor by power, but by My Spirit, Says the LORD of hosts." (Zech 4.6) We desire to be led by His Spirit and of His Spirit (Galatians 3:3). We want to stay clear of worldly programs and techniques in regard to the ministry.

#2 | "PRAYER IS THE BACKBONE OF THE MINISTRY" - 1 THESSALONIANS 5:17
"Pray without ceasing." (1 Thess. 5:17) The key to any spiritual success in the ministry is much prayer. It's once been said that the Church moves forward on Her knees. We pray a lot at Calvary Church.

#3 | "WORSHIP IS VITAL"- JOHN 4:24
"God is Spirit, and those who worship Him must worship in spirit and truth." (John 4:24) Spirit-led worship is vital at Calvary Church. Our worship is not just a time filler or a warm-up for the message. Our worship is a time set aside for the body to adore Him in all of His majesty.

#4 | "EMPHASIZE WHAT GOD HAS DONE FOR US NOT WHAT WE SHOULD DO FOR GOD" - EPHESIANS 1:3
"Blessed be the God and Father of our Lord Jesus Christ, who has blessed us with every spiritual blessing in the heavenly places in Christ" (Eph. 1:3) We seek to continually teach of the blessings of God, of all that He has done for us. We want to direct you past man to Jesus Christ (2 Cor. 4:7); not looking to, or dependent upon man but upon God alone.

#5 | "WHERE AND WHEN GOD GUIDES, HE PROVIDES" - PHILIPPIANS 4:19
"And my God shall supply all your need according to His riches in glory by Christ Jesus." (Phil. 4:19) We do not beg or present high-pressure sales techniques to raise money. We believe God will supply all of our financial needs and seek to be good stewards of His resources (Romans 12:11).

#6 | "YOU GOTTA BE THE SERVANT OF ALL" - MARK 10:45

"For even the Son of Man did not come to be served, but to serve, and to give His life a ransom for many." (Mark 10:45) Consistent servanthood was Jesus' style of ministry and so it must be ours (John 13:3-5). If we see something that needs to be done we can simply chip in and do it. The way up to God's Kingdom is to be a servant of all.

#7 | "WE MUST BE SUBMISSIVE AND UNCONDITIONALLY LOYAL TO GOD" - JAMES 4:7

"Therefore submit to God. Resist the devil and he will flee from you." (James 4:7) As we submit to our loving Heavenly Father, we seek to support those whom the Lord has put in authority. We desire to quickly resolve any problems that may arise so that we continue in unity serving the Lord.

#8 | "GOD WANTS INSPIRATION NOT PERSPIRATION" - 2 TIMOTHY 2:24

"And a servant of the Lord must not quarrel but be gentle to all, able to teach, patient...." (2 Tim. 2:24) God has a timing for His ministry and we desire to yield to His timing. We do not want to strive trying to knock through a door God has already closed. We always try to take steps of faith that are inspired by God.

#9 | "BLESSED ARE THE FLEXIBLE FOR THEY SHALL NOT BE BROKEN" - PROVERBS 3:5

"Trust in the LORD with all your heart, and lean not on your own understanding;." (Prov. 3:5) We seek to stay open and flexible to the things God desires to accomplish through us. Each Calvary Chapel is an independent vessel of the Lord free to biblically minister to each specific area of need.

#10 | "MINISTER TO OTHERS AND SEEK NOT TO BE MINISTERED TO" - EPHESIANS 4:11-12

"And He Himself gave some to be apostles, some prophets, some evangelists, and some pastors and teachers, for the equipping of the saints for the work of ministry, for the edifying of the body of Christ." (Eph. 4:12-13) Each member of God's family has special ministry gifts. We need to continually serve God with them, giving and ministering to others.

#11 | "WE ARE A MINISTRY TO ANYONE" - GALATIANS 3:28

"There is neither Jew nor Greek, there is neither slave nor free, there is neither male nor female; for you are all one in Christ Jesus." (Gal. 3:28) We desire to minister to everyone across the board; to anyone coming through the doors. As a fellowship, we are not a museum for saints but a hospital for the hurting. We want people to learn in a relaxed, comfortable, and informal yet respectable atmosphere.

#12 | "FEED THE FLOCK CONSISTENTLY VERSE BY VERSE, CHAPTER BY CHAPTER" - ACTS 20:27

"For I have not shunned to declare to you the whole counsel of God." (Acts 20:27) We desire to be a place where the Lord's sheep love to feed on the Word of God. God's Word is powerful so we teach it line upon line, verse-by-verse, chapter-by-chapter, book-by-book, and precept upon precept. We desire to know God through teaching His full counsel, the entire Bible.

#13 | "WE ARE THEOLOGICALLY BALANCED" - EPHESIANS 4:14

"...that we should no longer be children, tossed to and fro and carried about with every wind of doctrine, by the trickery of men, in the cunning craftiness of deceitful plotting." (Eph. 4:14) We desire to avoid doctrinal extremes. We're not just another church but a balanced body of believers seeking to be doctrinally sound, shying away from the present day extremes.

#14 | "HEALTHY SHEEP BEGET HEALTHY SHEEP" - ACTS 20:28

"Therefore take heed to yourselves and to all the flock, among which the Holy Spirit has made you overseers, to shepherd the church of God which He purchased with His own blood." (Acts 20:28) God honors His Word and increases the seeds that are planted by His sheep. When we teach the pure Word of God, it in turn develops a burden for the lost in the world. When God opens the doors, we go!

#15 | "WHEN CONFRONTED WITH SOMETHING WE DON'T UNDERSTAND, ALWAYS FALL BACK ON THAT WHICH WE DO UNDERSTAND" - PSALM 34:8

"Oh, taste and see that the LORD is good; Blessed is the man who trusts in Him!" (Psalm 34:8) We ought to always fall back on these foundational truths: (1) The Lord is Good, (2) God is Love, (3) Jesus is Lord, and (4) The Lord is ever present and will always be with you. As we hold fast to these truths, we'll find that the Lord will get us through anything. Calvary Chapel Aurora desires to be a ministry to the people, for the people, and by the people, all to the glory of God alone. We are excited that you are here and welcome you to make this your home church. Get plugged in and enjoy the movement of God in your life. You are truly loved!

OUR VALUES: Calvary Church Culture Statements

"THESE STATEMENTS DEFINE OUR CULTURE. KEEPING THE VISION OF CALVARY CHURCH CLEAR. EACH ONE REFLECTING OUR MUTUAL DEDICATION TO REACH PEOPLE WITH THE GOSPEL."

#1. We Love The Past, Live the Future
We celebrate what God has done in our past to prepare for what He is doing now and on into the future until He returns!

"But your eyes have seen every great act of the LORD which He did. Therefore you shall keep every commandment which I command you today, that you may be strong, and go in and possess the land which you cross over to possess, "and that you may prolong your days in the land which the LORD swore to give your fathers, to them and their descendants, 'a land flowing with milk and honey.'
Deut 11:7-9

It's fun to look back and see all the Lord has done. He has shown Himself faithful over and over again. But there is still new land up ahead, and we must look forward. The past cannot hinder us from moving forward with the Lord! Remember what God has done, but keep seeking what God wants to do.

#2 - We Embrace Change
We believe that God moves in many different ways; likewise, the leadership and vision that God provides doesn't always come in the same form. Creativity demands a certain level of change, and yet change needs to be focused and controlled. We embrace change and don't use the past as a crutch for the future. The message will not change, but the methods always will.

Then Jonathan said to the young man who bore his armor, "Come, let us go over to the garrison of these uncircumcised; it may be that the LORD will work for us. For nothing restrains the LORD from saving by many or by few." So his armorbearer said to him, "Do all that is in your heart. Go then; here I am with you, according to your heart."
1 Sam 14:6-7

The message of the gospel never changes. Jesus is the same yesterday, today, and forever. Yet methods change all the time. The methods we employ in spreading the gospel are adaptable to the needs in front of us. God has allowed us to enjoy new technologies, new innovative methods, and given His church extremely creative people to reach the lost. It's a good idea to try things out. Some will work. Some won't. But as long as we are being led by the Spirit, we can trust that He will use us! Embrace change. There will be a lot of changes in our fellowship until He returns!

#3 - We Follow the Leader

We are united as we fulfill the vision that God has given to Pastor Ed.

Jesus said to him, "If I will that he remain till I come, what is that to you? You follow Me." John 21:22

There is one, and only one Great Shepherd, Jesus Christ. He alone is our leader. He has given His Church one vision, His. Yet Jesus has chosen to convey delegated authority to pastors and leaders in His Church on the earth. Any good under-shepherd will follow the Good Shepherd. Where there is godly leadership, there is to be godly submission. We are to lovingly follow the leadership God has given to our pastor. Pastor Ed is here to edify the saints for the work of ministry. As our pastor follows Jesus, we follow along with his vision for Calvary.

#4 - We Lock Our Shields

We keep the battle on the outside and passionately defend against allowing it on the inside. We are united in battle!

For we do not wrestle against flesh and blood, but against principalities, against powers, against the rulers of the darkness of this age, against spiritual hosts of wickedness in the heavenly places. 13 Therefore take up the whole armor of God, that you may be able to withstand in the evil day, and having done all, to stand. Eph 6:12-13

Any army that fights needs unity based on authority to assure victory. The Roman army was known to lock their shields together so that they could make progress against the real enemies before them.
On our team, on our staff, among our fellowship, we don't choose to fight against each other. The real battle is not against each other but against the devil himself.

We want to do away with any petty skirmishes among us so that we might join forces for the Kingdom. We need to deal with things quickly. We need to stick up for each other. If you have an issue with a brother or sister, it's always the right thing to talk to them, and the wrong thing to talk about them. Like-mindedness is key in serving Jesus together.

#5 - We Are On His Mission

We will stop at nothing to accomplish our mission of pursuing a lost world.

"For the Son of Man has come to seek and to save that which was lost."
Luke 19:10

God has put us on the planet and in this community to reach the lost at any cost. Over the years we have done much to reach into our community with the love, mercy, and saving grace of Jesus Christ. We continue to see many saved, built up, and then sent out. Let's not forget why we are here. We are here to fulfill His mission. Jesus gave us a Great Commission, not a Great Suggestion! It's time to be bold and courageous in sharing the gospel.

#6 - We Are Dedicated To Doctrine

We are dedicated and committed to receiving and spreading good teaching. We want people to understand the depth of Scripture.

"But as for you, speak the things which are proper for sound doctrine."
Titus 2:1

We are committed to teaching the Bible from beginning to end, Genesis to Revelation, verse by verse and chapter by chapter. We are a textual community, one that is dedicated to the sound doctrine and expositional teaching of God's Word. Here at Calvary, a person will be fed the word of God in a steady spiritual diet. The Bible is alive and powerful and is the only source of truth from God. We are committed to sound teaching!

#7 - More Than A Song

We worship God energetically and passionately; it's not about the songs being sung but about Who they're being sung to. It can get loud, and it can be overwhelming, but we like it that way. Use your outside voice inside.

"Then I looked, and I heard the voice of many angels around the throne, the living creatures, and the elders; and the number of them was ten thousand times ten thousand, and thousands of thousands, saying with a loud voice: "Worthy is the Lamb who was slain To receive power and riches and wisdom, And strength and honor and glory and blessing!" Rev 5:11-12

We've always been committed to worshipping Jesus through song, music, and contemporary worship. With great variety, we sing together the glorious wonders of Jesus Christ! We sing for an audience of One! We are the choir and are not here to watch someone do something on the stage, but rather follow the worship leader into the very presence of God.

The Bible describes many different positions for worship, hands raised, kneeling down, even dancing! Sometimes it will be low key. Other times it will be loud and enthusiastic! I don't understand why some Christians think that enthusiasm is wrong and should not be in the sanctuary of the Lord! We worship Jesus in Spirit and in truth here excitedly and enthusiastically!

#8 - Our Fellowship Is For Anyone, Not Everyone

Our church is for anyone that will come, but we realize that not everyone likes the way we do things—and that's okay with us. We refuse to cater to personal preference in our pursuit of God, and while everyone is important to us, we are more concerned with reaching the lost than pacifying the critics.

"Can two walk together, unless they are agreed"? Amos 3:3

What a miserable journey it is walking with someone that is constantly disagreeing and disagreeable. God desires us to be of one mind and one accord!

It's unrealistic to think we will agree on everything; however, we will agree on most things. There is a beauty in diversity and an ugliness in divisiveness. There will be some disagreements along the way but not on major issues. Yet if this church family doesn't inspire you to worship Jesus, it's best to find another and go for it in Him! It's not God's will for you to be complaining all the time but worshipping all the time!

I love and appreciate the many good churches in our community and the Lord will put you where He needs you! We cannot and will not make changes just because someone doesn't like this or that, or we would be changing every week. Instead, we are following Jesus passionately and invite you on the journey!

#9 - We Are Not About The Numbers

Behind each number is a name and behind each hand is a heart.
It's not about how many people come to our church; it's about how many lives are changed.

"So continuing daily with one accord in the temple, and breaking bread from house to house, they ate their food with gladness and simplicity of heart, praising God and having favor with all the people. And the Lord added to the church daily those who were being saved." Acts 2:46-47

When God makes Calvary your spiritual home, we want you to encounter Him here! Sure you will connect with others, do life together, and serve people, but what you really need is a true encounter with God.
We've seen incredible growth here over the years. We are no longer a fellowship of 30 meeting in the basement of a rented Baptist Church. Yet in our growth, we are trusting Jesus to build His church, one by one.
You're important God. He knows you by name, knows how many hairs are on your head, or not! It's not about numbers here as much as it's about individuals, people connected and encountering God!

#10 - We Make Room For Growth

We're not so blind to believe that we have it all together or that the way we do things is the only way—the same way isn't always the right way. We are always looking for new ways to grow, and we support creative thinking.

"But grow in the grace and knowledge of our Lord and Savior Jesus Christ. To Him be the glory both now and forever. Amen. 2 Peter 3:18

We're all growing an in the process of being conformed into the very image of Christ. We are all on a spiritual journey, all in the place of sanctification. We are learning how to please God and obey Him better. We are open to learn from other ministries, other ministers, and other believers. He wants us to continue in our spiritual growth until we see Him face to face. God has provided teams of godly men and women who work collaboratively together seeking to fulfill His purposes through our church family. Thank God He's growing us up together in Him!

#11 - It's Not A Job

We believe that God has called us to serve Him regardless of rank or title, and we believe that each person in the church has a role to play in this work. We are called to this ministry whether there is a paycheck or not. It's not a job; it's a calling.

"And I thank Christ Jesus our Lord who has enabled me, because He counted me faithful, putting me into the ministry.." 1 Tim 1:12

Whether your paycheck is signed by the US Government, or UPS, or Calvary Church, you are a real true minister of God! Serve Him as such. We are all important parts of the Body of Christ. Find out what God has called you to do... and do it!

#12 - We Cultivate A Culture Of Honor

We believe that Jesus lived a life of honor: honoring the Father, honoring others, and receiving honor Himself. We operate on this same model: Honor Up (the Lord and those in leadership over us), Honor Out (those who serve alongside of us), Honor All-Around (those we serve with, all guests, and those we come into contact with). We honor freely without inhibition, realizing that it's not as much about people deserving honor as it is about us living a life of honor and creating a culture of honor.

"Honor all people. Love the brotherhood. Fear God. Honor the king." 1 Peter 2:17

We want to treat each other in love as royalty. Love, respect, and honor help to move the Church along the path in a dark and desperate world. Everyone, no matter what, deserves respect.

#13 - We Passionately Pursue A Faith Walk

We set unattainable goals and then trust in an unstoppable God. We put it all on the line trusting that God is working behind the scenes. We don't want to be safe; we want to take risks.

"But without faith it is impossible to please Him, for he who comes to God must believe that He is, and that He is a rewarder of those who diligently seek Him." Heb 11:6

Rather than staying in the place of safety and security, we desire to launch out into the deep to see what God wants to do! We love to venture out in faith. Ask God for a spiritual dream, a big dream, and then pursue Him! Go for it and watch for His fruit to come!

#14 - Generosity Multiplies Capacity

We encourage a culture of generous giving. We give obediently to God, according to His call, and we give generously, according to our hearts. Our vision for ministry always exceeds our capacity for ministry. But we believe that if each of us takes the responsibility of stewardship personally, God will multiply our means and provide the capacity to do things that may seem impossible.

"Therefore I thought it necessary to exhort the brethren to go to you ahead of time, and prepare your generous gift beforehand, which you had previously promised, that it may be ready as a matter of generosity and not as a grudging obligation." 2 Cor 9:5

There is a great joy in partnering together for the work of the ministry. Our capacity to reach more people increases as the generosity of our fellowship grows. Remember, you can't out give God. He owns it all. Step out in faithfulness in your giving and watch what the Lord wants to do!

Made in the USA
Columbia, SC
17 September 2022

67279330R00065